LIVING of ADVENT & the CHRISTMAS SEASON

2 · 0 · 0 · 4

Aidan R. Rooney, C.M.

Paulist Press
New York/Mahwah, N.J.

Scripture quotations are from the *New Revised Standard Version of the Bible,* copyright 1989 by the Division of Christian Education of the National Council of Churches of Christ in the U.S.A. All rights reserved. Used by permission.

Copyright © 2004 by the Congregation of the Mission of Saint Vincent de Paul in Germantown, PA.

Illustrated by Sr. Ellen M. LaCapria, D.C.

Original poetry © by Br. Augustine D. Towey, C.M. Used by kind permission of the author:
"The Advent" from *Waiting for Snow in Lewiston* (Lewiston, NY: Mellen Poetry Press, 1990)
"When Christ Comes" from *Later Enchantments* (Francestown, NH: Typographeum Press, 2000)
"You Are a Word God Utters to Me" from *The Things of Man* (Lewiston, NY: Mellen Poetry Press, 1991)
"Ice Storm" from *Silences* (Lewiston, NY: Mellen Poetry Press, 1996)

All rights reserved. No part of this book may be reproduced or transmitted in any form or by any means, electronic or mechanical, including photocopying, recording, or by any information storage and retrieval system without permission in writing from the Publisher.

ISBN: 0-8091-4239-2

Published by Paulist Press
997 Macarthur Boulevard
Mahwah, New Jersey 07430

www.paulistpress.com

Printed and bound in the
United States of America

Introduction

"Dearest, all that remains is that you find your way."
"You are a word God utters to me."

These two lines of the poetry of Brother Augustine D. Towey, C.M. have come to hold for me the beauty and the power of the Advent-Christmas cycle. The mysteries of these two seasons are all wrapped up in what is meant when we say, "God loves us," as we begin to tell the tale of that love through the liturgical year. Our tradition has always insisted, in prayer and teaching, in art and song, that this is a love made real in flesh and blood

What I have tried to do in wedding the words of a poet with the contours of the seasonal scriptures is to provide a window into the mysteries we celebrate. Sometimes this window is clear–the reflection of many years. Sometimes, less so, because it is recent reflection, or because it is a piece of the mystery with which I still struggle. I am grateful to Brother Augustine for allowing me to employ his poetry in this way.

To this world of poetry and prose, I have invited the perceptive hand of artist Sister Ellen M. LaCapria, D.C. Sister Ellen, working with the same poetry and scripture, and without seeing my reflections, produced the drawings that you will find throughout this little book. She is, in the language that she has mastered, a coauthor of this work.

And so, the three of us, a daughter and two sons of St. Vincent de Paul, invite you to contemplate the mystery of a God who takes flesh amongst the poorest of the poor.

–Aidan R. Rooney, C.M.

Sunday, November 28
First Sunday of Advent

. . . You know what time it is, how it is now the moment for you to wake from sleep. For salvation is nearer to us now. . . .
Romans 13:11

Why *now*? Was salvation so far away from me throughout the rest of the year? I almost resent the coming of this season, with its challenging, its reminding, its almost chiding nature. Make room for his coming! Wake from your sleep! You cannot know the day of the Lord's coming! Stop!

These are, sometimes, the hardest days of this season. The shifting days. The world lurches ahead. Our faith says, "Stay still, stay sharp, hold back." I try my best to be attentive to your presence, Lord, this day and every day. Yet you ask, "More: deeper, my child. Draw down. Rest." You've caught us again, O God, between the world and your reign. Our hearts are drawn in both directions, and I'm finding it so difficult to do what you ask. But, I'm here. I'm willing.

I have prepared for your coming what I can prepare.
I've cleared my desk of business and my heart
Is empty. Tests are graded and whatever part
Of me possible stands ready as if on a stair.
from "The Advent"

Monday, November 29
First Week of Advent

On that day, the branch of the Lord shall be beautiful and glorious. . . .
Isaiah 4:2a

This is the dream of Advent, and preparing for a dream takes a special kind of work. What I've learned about this time of year is to try not to be so sensitive. I know my life is not in the order it should be. But God's promise is still offered to me.

First things first: accept the *reality* of the offer. God wants me to live in a world made new. God wants me to live in a world of peace and compassion and justice and mercy. But if I don't see a hint of it in the here and now, how can I hope?

Do the work. Learn to see more deeply. Pay attention to the world, for the signs you seek are there. Start small. Clear the desk of a busy life. Empty your heart of the clutter of past hurts and fixed expectations.

Lord, help me to at least slow down a little today, so that I might notice the signs of your coming. Help me to see your presence when it covers me as

. . . a shade by day from the heat, and a refuge and a shelter from the storm and rain.
Isaiah 4:6

Tuesday, November 30
Saint Andrew

So faith comes from what is heard, and what is heard comes through the word of Christ. *Romans 10:17*

As the Advent season gets underway, Andrew's feast day reminds us that there is still work to be done. Although life will get fairly busy in the next few weeks—if it isn't already—followers of Jesus still have the responsibility to be heralds of the Good News. One of the struggles of this first week of Advent is to remember that for us, following him is what it's all about.

A lot of the "heart work" of this season involves keeping track of our own energy. Is it joy and love that drives the shopping and the preparing, or is it anxiety? Paul's letter to the Church in Rome invites us to trust that Jesus saves. Our activities of the season can have a holiness to them, if they come from a holy place within us. We can be a "word of Christ" if we radiate the joy of preparation. An excited expectation rooted in love looks a lot different to family and neighbors than the frantic, anxiety-ridden heart already crushed under the weight of "finding the right gift!"

. . . How beautiful are the feet of those who bring good news! *Romans 10:15b*

Wednesday, December 1
First Week of Advent

On this mountain the LORD of hosts will make for all peoples a feast of rich food, a feast of well-aged wines, of rich food filled with marrow, of well-aged wines strained clear.
Isaiah 25:6

Don't stop at the first verse. Read Isaiah 25:6–10. Set that vision in your heart for this whole season. Reflect on it. Long for it. Count on it. Whenever you encounter something that doesn't match it, say to yourself, "There's work to be done to get this to where God wants it."

The pictures that the prophets paint are meant to stir us to hope-filled action. If I don't have a vision, my hope in a joyful future can wane when faced with the realities of the world. Even the pettiness and triviality of some of my own day-to-day life can eat away at my hope. If I'm serious about preparing for Christ in my life, I've got to know the world that he hopes for. I've got to learn to love what he loves.

He comes to set the feast. Rich food and fine wines. Is that what I want? Or am I satisfied with unremarkable everyday fare?

Lord, give me the longing for the richness of your reign.

And all of them ate and were filled; and they took up the broken pieces left over, seven baskets full.
Matthew 15:37

Thursday, December 2
First Week of Advent

> Trust in the Lord forever, for in the LORD GOD you have an everlasting rock. For he has brought low the inhabitants of the height; the lofty city he lays low. *Isaiah 26:4-5a*

Advent is a hard season. As our minds drift "Christmasward," the church uses Isaiah's unruly tongue to get our attention. As if the world wasn't having a hard enough time!

That's just it. The world *is* having a hard time, and part of the preparation of this season is knowing how true that is, and, at the same moment, knowing that God has different hopes for the world. God has made some promises. Prophets have painted some pictures. A people that longs for Christ also longs for the world made new. We can't ignore the world's dying, its injustice, its war. See the dying. See the rising. It's that Easter *presence,* right here, right now, as I'm getting ready for Christmas.

Isaiah and Matthew tell us not to be afraid to see the world clearly. God is straightening the way for the just. Trust God.

> "The rains fell, the floods came, and the winds blew and beat on that house, but it did not fall, because it had been founded on rock." *Matthew 7:25*

Friday, December 3
Saint Francis Xavier

On that day, the deaf shall hear the words of a scroll, and out of their gloom and darkness the eyes of the blind shall see. The meek shall obtain fresh joy in the LORD, and the neediest people shall exult in the Holy One of Israel.
Isaiah 29:18-19

Where can I see this happening today? This is part of the "work" of preparation in Advent. Read the newspapers more thoroughly. Don't get caught up by the merely shocking; dig for the good stuff! *Where* is God at work? It may be difficult to find. Sometimes God's work doesn't sell newspapers.

If you can't see God's work happening, begin to make the promises of Isaiah in your own words. God can "make a way out of no way." Sometimes, my inability to see God working is a result of my refusal to expect God to do what God has promised. If I really want reconciliation in the world, dare I hope for it in my own relationships? Have I tried to settle any rifts I know of?

Lord, help me to hope actively and to act hopefully.

Then he touched their eyes and said, "According to your faith, let it be done to you." *Matthew 9:29*

Saturday, December 4
Saint John of Damascus

Then Jesus summoned his twelve disciples and gave them authority over unclean spirits, to cast them out, and to cure every disease and every sickness. *Matthew 10:1*

Every disease and *every* sickness? This is one of the many places where I struggle. I'm willing to allow for *small* triumphs, but my faith falters in the face of the powerful statements of the gospels. Part of the preparation that the Advent season requires is the willingness to allow the visions of the scriptures to enlarge our faith. That begins not so much by staring at our own lack of faith, but beginning to look around more and more.

The evidence for the power of God will always be limited if I spend most of my energy staring at myself. One of the special seductions of the Adversary is to convince me that I will forever be in the way of my own spiritual growth. The call of the gospel is to go out and *do* the things that I long to see. Faith grows in the wake of faith acted upon. God is able. I can count on God's power. I can act as if the visions of the prophets are true.

As you go, proclaim the good news, "The kingdom of heaven has come near." Cure the sick, raise the dead, cleanse the lepers, cast out demons. *Matthew 10:7-8*

Sunday, December 5
Second Sunday of Advent

> A shoot shall come out from the stump of Jesse. . . . He shall not judge by what his eyes see . . . but with righteousness he shall judge the poor, and decide with equity for the meek of the earth. . . .
> *Isaiah 11:1a,4a*

My expectations are high this year for a better year than last year. But again the hopes are focused on *me*. The trouble with this season is that it mixes things up all the time. The subtle draw of the babe in the manger can almost stupefy me, almost make me forget the larger world and its needs. Carols are seemingly sung by sirens; that's what's going on. Your concerns and your dreams are so much mightier than mine, O God. How did you become so fearless? How can you still see the world of which your Prophet spoke? Are you looking at the same thing I am?

I know you are on the way, Lord, and here I am again, gingerly pruning my life to make room for you, knowing all too well that there are things that might need a heavier hand taken to them. I'm not sure what you want of me, so I'm starting with the simple things, trusting that you will lead me deeper in these weeks to come. Saint Paul said you are "steadfast." Please be patient once more, my friend, my God.

> *I will come down to greet you at the door.*
> *Until then I've balanced budgets and my gifts*
> *Are wrapped. I've tried to settle any rifts*
> *I know of. I hear you on the porch's broken floor.*
> from "The Advent"

Monday, December 6
Saint Nicholas

The wilderness and the dry land shall be glad, the desert shall rejoice and blossom; like the crocus it shall blossom abundantly, and rejoice with joy and singing.

Isaiah 35:1-2a

Read all of Isaiah 35 today. *Twice.* This is the abundance that God wants to share. People get healed; peace is the normal state of affairs. The earth's bounty is available for everyone and at no charge!

It's wonderful that these images happen to coincide with the feast of old Saint Nick. A more generous fellow you never met. Caring for the poor, leaving presents . . . Meaning no disrespect, but St. Nicholas doesn't even come close to what God has in store for us, if we would just open our eyes and our hearts.

Only a closed heart could call healing "blasphemy," but it shouldn't surprise us that the early church had as much trouble with closed hearts as we do. God's love never ends; it rains on the just and the unjust. Why is that so hard to accept? Part of preparing is just getting used to the idea of the world that God wants. The rocks and the dirt sing!

. . . they shall obtain joy and gladness, and sorrow and sighing shall flee away. *Isaiah 35:10b*

Tuesday, December 7
Saint Ambrose

Comfort, O comfort my people, says your God. Speak tenderly to Jerusalem, and cry to her that she has served her term, that her penalty is paid, that she has received from the Lord's hand double for all her sins.   *Isaiah 40:1-2*

Being set free. I have a friend who is a prison chaplain, and sometimes talks with men who are never getting out of jail. *Ever!* What they talk about is how to be free *inside.* I think that's harder work, sometimes—not to be compelled by anything I can't name.

It seems to me that the surest road to that kind of freedom is to set others free. Working for justice on local, national and international fronts is part of the preparation, too. Struggling to make a world that resembles the world that Isaiah envisioned—that's part of the call of this season. And it's the antidote to the self-centeredness that makes me blind to the presence of God in my world.

God, give me the strength to engage the world in its brokenness. Take me out of myself and toward the world you love.

Get you up to a high mountain, O Zion, herald of good tidings; lift up your voice with strength, O Jerusalem, herald of good tidings, lift it up, do not fear. . . .   *Isaiah 40:9*

WEDNESDAY, DECEMBER 8
IMMACULATE CONCEPTION

And he came to her and said, "Greetings, favored one! The Lord is with you." . . . Then Mary said, "Here am I, the servant of the Lord; let it be with me according to your word."
Luke 1:28, 38

Greetings, indeed! Mary is pivotal. To preparing. To understanding. To living. This is a good season to get to know Our Lady, the Blessed Mother.

In strength, and in a calm, graced assertion, salvation finds its "yes." What was her life like—her inner life I mean—the life that counts. What made her that ready?

She became a servant without losing herself. She wasn't some "vessel" simply used by God. She was a free partner. How did she get to know God well enough to make that relationship work?

Her continued, God-given, Spirit-driven presence arrives again and again in devotions, encounters, and medals miraculous.

This is a good season to get to know her. God loved her and chose her, as God loved and chose us

. . . before the foundation of the world. . . .
Ephesians 1:4

THURSDAY, DECEMBER 9
SAINT JUAN DIEGO

When the poor and needy seek water, and there is none, and their tongue is parched with thirst, I the LORD will answer them, I the God of Israel will not forsake them. I will open rivers on the bare heights, and fountains in the midst of valleys. . . .   *Isaiah 41:17-18a*

The poor have always been special to God. The needy and those who in their distress cry out to God. They have learned the folly of self-sufficiency, and the humility of dependence on God. The well-to-do, like me, have a lot to learn.

Is part of the problem in getting into this season my own self-sufficiency? Do I have trouble longing for the coming of a Savior because I really do put my ultimate trust in *myself*? If this is true, no wonder I can't perceive God's activity. My inflated self is blocking the view!

Simple Juan Diego. He just opened himself to the gift.

Lord, I am still too fearful to ask you to make me poor in fact. Make me poor in spirit, longing only for you.

For I, the Lord your God, hold your right hand; it is I who say to you, "Do not fear, I will help you."   *Isaiah 41:13*

Friday, December 10
Second Week of Advent

"But to what will I compare this generation? It is like children sitting in the marketplaces and calling to one another, 'we played the flute for you, and you did not dance. . . .'"
Matthew 11:16-17

How obtuse I can be! Some days I begin to wonder if I really do want to meet Christ in my life. Jesus' critique of his "generation" could easily be applied today.

Actually, it doesn't sound like a critique these days. It's more like a lament—"Would you please look for me?" "What kind of sign do you need?" In preparing to celebrate the Christmas mystery, I can almost miss the point. God calls out "See me! Meet me! Travel with me!" Preparing or making ready means accepting who God wants to be in my life.

Lord, if you will show yourself to me on this day, I will try to be attentive to your presence. Don't let my sinfulness get in the way. Repair what is broken; heal what is hurt.

I am the Lord your God, . . . who leads you in the way you should go. *Isaiah 48:17b*

Saturday, December 11
Pope Damasus I

Then Elijah arose, a prophet like fire, and his word burned like a torch.
Sirach 48:1

Not that the prophet Elijah's words burned things, rather, they illumined what was there. The problem is that no one wanted to look at what could be seen by the light of Elijah's torch. John the Baptist's words had the same effect.

Part of preparing is having a good look at all the sin, all the dirt. Here's where Advent gets a little like Lent. Preparation means repentance and reform, as well as expectation and longing. There's a sacrament for this; it's called *penance*.

It is also true that what keeps anxiety alive, what crushes real hope, is the wounded part of ourselves. Sin isn't always something we've done; sometimes it's something that's been done to us. It needs to be looked at so it can be healed. Preparation means seeking the help we need in order to heal. There's a community for this; it's called *church*.

Lord, we want you to love us, to change us, to heal us, but sometimes we're afraid to let you do it. Give us the courage to stand in the light of Elijah's torch!

Happy are those who saw you and were adorned with your love! For we also shall surely live. *Sirach 48:11*

Sunday, December 12
Third Sunday of Advent

... "Go and tell John what you hear and see: the blind receive their sight, the lame walk, the lepers are cleansed, the deaf hear, the dead are raised and the poor have good news brought to them." *Matthew 11:4-5*

I can't remember when I decided that getting ready for you, Lord, was a project—when it had ceased to be a joy. But that's where life had led me. I actually went through a time when I wanted to deny myself carols, parties, even the Holy Babe. And then it dawned on me, and I realized you had been speaking to me in more than one tongue, more than one language. You wanted me to look at the world with the same love, the same feeling with which I gaze upon the Holy Babe. Then I would see the world as you see it, and have the hope you want me to have. I had struggled to avoid you as the infant in the manger, for that was too small and sentimental. I had feared to meet you in the power of your coming in glory. I had been caught between your advents.

I've shoveled the walk of snow till it is bare,
And if no other storms should occur I should
Be safe. A single deer at the edge of the wood
Stomps and stares. Nights have been colder, but days fair.
from "The Advent"

Monday, December 13
Saint Lucy

I see him, but not now; I behold him, but not near—
a star shall come out of Jacob, and a scepter shall
rise out of Israel. . . . *Numbers 24:17a*

The beginning of real sight is expectation. Something coalesces deep within you that allows you to believe a promise is true. Then, you gaze expectantly into the present and see his future coming.

It sounds contradictory: how can I see the future by staring intently at the present? But think through why you can hold the Christ of Bethlehem, the Christ of your life today, and the Christ who is Lord of all creation in your heart. Stories of the Babe in the manger stirred your faith. You began to look for him in the here and now. Finding him today allows hope for the future.

So look deeply into today. You may find, perhaps, only a glimmer of Christ. It could be the kindness of a friend. It could be your own kindness. It could be the struggle of nations to find peace. It could be the suffering of peoples without peace. I know it's difficult. But we must look, and declare what we see. The divine is here, now, always.

St. Lucy will help you see clearly, if you ask in faith, to become someone

". . . whose eye is clear, . . . one who hears the words of God, and knows the knowledge of the Most High, who sees the vision of the Almighty, who falls down, but with his eyes uncovered: . . ." *Numbers 24:15-16*

Tuesday, December 14
Saint John of the Cross

Jesus said to them,
"Truly I tell you,
the tax collectors
and the prostitutes
are going into the kingdom
of God ahead of you."
Matthew 21:31b

This is the part of the picture that's hard to take. A wag once said that God had pretty high hopes but very low standards. I count on that. Don't you?

The toughest part of this, the part we resist, is not who gets in, or even who gets in first. It's that God wants to tinker with our hearts. To change them. Perhaps fix them. To heal them. God wants to get very, very close to a place inside that no one ever gets to. It is simply hard to take. Overwhelming, really. God *wants* you. God wants *you*.

Mystics like John of the Cross edged up close to this place inside and called it "dark." Our dominant culture tells us this kind of "dark" can be frightening. But it is also the touch of a father's hand, gently comforting his child, or of a mother's arms wrapped tightly around her newborn child.

On that day, you shall not be put to shame because of all the deeds by which you have rebelled against me. . . .
Zephaniah 3:11a

Wednesday, December 15
Third Week of Advent

By myself I have sworn, from my mouth has gone forth in righteousness a word that shall not return: "To me every knee shall bow, every tongue shall swear." *Isaiah 45:23*

Preparing for the coming of the Lord in the *flesh* seems only slightly more baffling than preparing for the coming of the Lord in any way whatsoever. This is the eternal God that I await. Who am I kidding? Saints wait that way, not me.

If I really lived in expectation of the coming of the Lord I would, to paraphrase Annie Dillard, have my crash-helmet on!

If I allow myself to become calm, I can know that the God for whom I long really can be a deep comfort. Surely, it is also a threat to this soul, but it is a comfort to acknowledge that this world is in God's gentle embrace.

As you count the number of things left to be done (there are only ten days left until Christmas), turn to God and be safe. In a moment of restfulness in this Advent season, encourage your heart to long for God alone.

> **. . . there is no other.**
> *Isaiah 45:22b*

Thursday, December 16
Third Week of Advent

Do not fear, for you will not be ashamed; do not be discouraged, for you will not suffer disgrace. *Isaiah 54:4a*

Fear.

God knows it can crowd out possibility. How many times in the story of Christ's coming does God say "Do not be afraid!"?

When I start to trust that God is active and present in the world, it becomes a less fear-provoking place. That's why the prophet's words are so important. If we don't forget that God is holding history, although it swerves in its recklessness, trust remains steady.

Christmas is just around the corner. The promise of Christ born among us invites me to a renewed and deeper trust.

Lord, I become afraid so easily, because life hasn't always proved trustworthy. At least you've never failed. Help me to trust you at all times. You keep sending messengers into my life.

. . . with everlasting love, I will have compassion on you, says the Lord, your Redeemer. *Isaiah 54:8b*

Friday, December 17
Third Week of Advent

So all the generations from Abraham to David are fourteen generations; and from David to the deportation to Babylon, fourteen generations; and from the deportation to Babylon to the Messiah, fourteen generations. *Matthew 1:17*

Tamar, Ruth, the wife of Uriah, Mary. These are the special women of Jesus' lineage. If you have the eyes to see, there's something here. I don't propose to tell anyone what that something is. It does tell a particular truth for this season's journey, though: If you pay attention to the irregularities, you might have a better chance of noticing God. And you have more questions than when you started.

At this point in Advent, the scriptures and the church turn with more intention toward the coming of Christ in the flesh. God in the flesh: now there's a colossal irregularity. And so, we pay attention, and start cataloging our questions. What does it mean to say God dwells among us? In the flesh? Flesh of a prostitute named Tamar. Flesh of a virgin named Mary.

Lord, deepen in me the spirit of contemplation for this part of the journey. Help me to begin at the beginning. Who is this Jesus that I await?

Abraham was the father of Isaac, and Isaac the father of Jacob, and Jacob the father of Judah. . . . *Matthew 1:2*

Saturday, December 18
Third Week of Advent

In his days Judah will be saved and Israel will live in safety. And this is the name by which he will be called: "The Lord is our righteousness." *Jeremiah 23:6*

Someone running the show: that's what we're looking for. It seems to have been the longing of hearts throughout time. We all want to know that if we lean back, it will be into arms we can trust.

Well, we can. God is with us. The Lord. Adonai.

These last days before the Christmas season invite us to begin to contemplate nothing but God-with-us. Even the scriptures today "get ahead of themselves." You'd swear it was Christmas morning. If we're paying attention, it is.

Emmanuel.

"Look, the virgin shall conceive and bear a son, and they shall name him Emmanuel," which means, "God is with us."
Matthew 1:23

Sunday, December 19
Fourth Sunday of Advent

Therefore the Lord himself will give you a sign. Look, the young woman is with child and shall bear a son, and shall name him Immanuel.   *Isaiah 7:14*

You have made room where I thought there was none. My life that I thought so full just needed to have the debris cleared away. Your challenges have let me forget my own riotous life, and look around for the hints of your presence. Peace glints. Justice sighs like a baby sleeping. Because of the words you spoke this season, I thought your coming would be louder somehow.

Preparing has sometimes been a struggle. Your love has carried me, corrected me when necessary. I'm going to spend these last few days training my ear and my eye. I'll live with your Word, as it shouts from the scriptures, as it nips in the crisp air, as it fights its way through the noise of the news on CNN. I know what to look for. I know what to listen for: "Peace is coming. Justice dawns. The virgin shall conceive. Do not be afraid."

> *I've set aside what might encumber your stay.*
> *My calendar is free of lunches, meetings.*
> *There is none left to whom I must send greetings.*
> *Dearest, all that remains is that you find your way.*
>   from "The Advent"

Monday, December 20
Fourth Week of Advent

"The Holy Spirit will come upon you, and the power of the Most High will overshadow you. . . ." *Luke 1:35a*

    This stunning, direct statement opens up a whole new world. More than just a God who accompanies, more than a God who intervenes, this is a God who joins, invents, transforms, caresses.

    The meeting is so brief in Luke's account.

> An enigmatic greeting.
>   An assurance.
>   An announcement.
>   A question.
>   An answer.
>   A vow.
>   A quickening.

    Confounding! Yet, the poet calls out "Dearest" to the Expected One. The dialogues of Christmas are lovers' dialogues. Creator and creation, fathers and mothers, mother and child, lover and beloved.

But she was much perplexed by his words and pondered what sort of greeting this might be. *Luke 1:29*

Tuesday, December 21
Fourth Week of Advent

The voice of the beloved! Look, he comes, leaping upon the mountains, bounding over the hills. *The Song of Songs 2:8*

Breathless movement characterizes these days in scripture and in life. The Word suggests anticipation, and the flushing of the lover's cheek. In *my* world, it's more like crazed darting about from store to store.

It seems that it will be impossible again this year to remain calm during this final week of Advent. How shall I claim the day for myself and my Beloved? If I pay attention to my body, its tensions and relaxations, the racing of the heartbeat as I run from mall to mall, I can offer it to the One who comes. My breathlessness, begun in anxiety, then becomes a prayer.

> *He leans forward*
> *Prepared to dust my heart,*
> *But the drum in my heart is still talking,*
> *And the drum in my heart is still talking,*
>
> *And he says, "Hello,"*
> *And the drum stills,*
>
> *And the stillness is clean.*

from "When Christ Comes"

Wednesday, December 22
Fourth Week of Advent

"My soul magnifies the Lord, and my spirit rejoices in God my Savior, for he has looked with favor on the lowliness of his servant." *Luke 1:47-48a*

Hannah and Miriam. Pregnant women. Busy women. Faithful women. Occupied by God. Engaged by the world. Self-possessed in their relation to each.

Learn from these women. In creative and assertive self-care, each of them keeps a "respectful distance" from both God and world. There is no false intimacy: God is still "Lord" and "Mighty One," to be offered praise and the recounting of deeds. There is no cheap romance about the world; it is still a place of mixed motives, mixed justice, and mixed results.

Dealing with "life on life's terms," someone once said. God is God, the world is the world, and I am who I am. It's a peaceful way to live. Always prepared. Always remembering.

He scattered the proud. Brought down the powerful. Lifted up the lowly. Filled the hungry. Sent the rich away. Helped his servant. Name the days, times, and places when this was true.

"My heart exults in the Lord; my strength is exalted in my God. My mouth derides my enemies, because I rejoice in my victory." *1 Samuel 2:1*

Thursday, December 23
Fourth Week of Advent

But who can endure the day of his coming, and who can stand when he appears? For he is like a refiner's fire. . . .
Malachi 3:2

Get ready! Emmanuel is almost here. The "messenger" of Malachi, Elijah, John the Baptist is giving us one final call. Open your eyes, your ears, your hearts. What you have longed for appears.

Even the church gets breathless at this point. But this is the excitement of true hope. If our preparation has been lax, he will visit us anyway. We'll accept what we are prepared to accept. He gives himself freely.

These are days of wonder, these days that surround the feast, best lived if our bodies are rested and our spirits awake. That's hard to achieve if there are young ones in the family and busy schedules at work. But even in the rush of these last days, our Advent preparations have tuned us in to the places of Christ's coming: the love, the giving, the feasts, the joyful songs, the remembering. Today's response to the psalm at Eucharist says it all:

". . . stand up and raise your heads, because your redemption is drawing near." *Luke 21:28*

Friday, December 24
Fourth Week of Advent

"By the tender mercy of our God, the dawn from on high will break upon us, to give light to those who sit in darkness and in the shadow of death, to guide our feet into the way of peace."   *Luke 1:78–79*

This morning could be sublimely quiet, riotously frantic, or it could be just like any other morning. Stop for a moment. What is your heart saying today? Are you ready to greet him? If we have succeeded in preparation, no matter what the pace of life at this point, we can be assured that God holds our life, gently and firmly. The affirmative language of Luke is so stirring: the dawn from on high *will* break upon us. There are very few things outside of ourselves that we can know with assurance, but this is one of them. He is coming. *To* us. *For* us.

I've shoveled the walk of snow till it is bare,
And if no other storms should occur I should
Be safe. A single deer at the edge of the wood
Stomps and stares. Nights have been colder, but
   days fair.

I've set aside what might encumber your stay.
My calendar is free of lunches, meetings.
There is none left to whom I must send greetings.
Dearest, all that remains is that you find your way.

from "The Advent"

Saturday, December 25
Nativity of the Lord

And the word became flesh and lived among us, and we have seen his glory, the glory as of a father's only son, full of grace and truth. *John 1:14*

This day came almost before I was ready, because you had swept me up into the waiting. Thank you, O God, for turning me toward your world and its people, the strangers and the friends, the poor and the rich, the hard earth and the brittle grass.

I have often longed to recover the excitement that this day held when I was a child. Do you remember how hard it was to go to sleep with one eye open? You just knew something wonderful was on the way.

And now it's here. Everywhere! Welcome to a season that begs us to live with both eyes wide open!

> *You are a word God utters to me,*
> *Neither lie, nor random, nor a second thought.*
>
> *You are his diction, accent, definition,*
> *God's verb, His lyric, His conversation,*
> *His rhythm, His rhyme.*
>
> *You are a word God utters to me,*
> *And I am a word with which He answers you.*

from "You Are a Word God Utters to Me"

Sunday, December 26
The Holy Family

As God's chosen ones, holy and beloved, clothe yourselves with compassion, kindness, humility, meekness, and patience. Bear with one another and, . . . forgive each other. . . .
Colossians 3:12–13a

The day after, and there couldn't be a better word. It's something to think about. The first "feast" after Christmas reminds us that, in most households, someone is bound to come to waken us a bit too early. Life has presented itself no different from the day before: full of wonder, full of flesh and blood. My dream comes true, but not in the way I expected. Whoever is family to me is here, and is holy.

In the darkness of my room
At night
This is what I see:

Christ walks through
The windows.
First the venetian blinds
Whip up like an act curtain,

And the curtains
Billow in,
Floating up toward the ceiling.

from "When Christ Comes"

Monday, December 27
Saint John the Evangelist

We declare to you what was from the beginning, what we have heard, what we have seen with our eyes, what we have looked at and touched with our hands, concerning the word of life. . . . *1 John 1:1*

All this week, we can spend our time basking in the warmth of Christmas. If we weren't too sure, John reminds us that God is revealed in flesh and blood. The eternal God dwells with us.

Look around at the people with whom you share life. Was God revealed to you in them these past few days? Did you consider that God would be there?

Have you sensed the permanence and solidity of your relationship with God in Christ?

For many this season of the year is tinged with loss. Have you been assured that those you have loved are not lost? Have you visited a cemetery and not felt bereft, but quietly joyful amidst your sadness? Sometimes, that's how he comes. As soft comfort for the first time.

Then the other disciple, who reached the tomb first, also went in, and he saw and believed. . . . *John 20:8*

Tuesday, December 28
The Holy Innocents

This is the message we have heard from him and proclaim to you, that God is light and in him there is no darkness at all.
1 John 1:5

It's a sobering thought that one reaction to the birth of the child Jesus is the murder of hundreds of innocent children by King Herod. The word spoken is a revealing word, a word of truth. Elijah's torch is still here.

There's something in me that wants this reality to go away. I don't want to know the sinfulness of the world this close to Christmas. I want only words of joy and light and goodness. It is truly a weary world that rejoices in the coming of the Lord. The deep truth of this season is revealed starkly today. Christ comes into the real world, to love and to save. His passion is never too far away.

. . . he is the atoning sacrifice for our sins, and not for ours only but also for the sins of the whole world. *1 John 2:2*

Wednesday, December 29
Fifth Day in the Octave of Christmas

Whoever says, "I have come to know him," but does not obey his commandments, is a liar, and in such a person the truth does not exist; but whoever obeys his word, truly in this person the love of God has reached perfection. By this we may be sure that we are in him: whoever says, "I abide in him," ought to walk just as he walked. *1 John 2:4-6*

Once we've let him in, we have the power and the responsibility to live as he asks. These weeks, devoted to the first letter of John, lay out the expectations, and the firmness of our hope.

First things first, says the author: love is what you have been given, love is what is expected. Don't be stingy, and don't worry that you'll run out. You are not asked to do something that you don't know how to do, or that you haven't heard about before. But now there's no backing away. Give the gift you have been given.

His presence is revealed not simply as comfort, but with a purpose—that all people might be drawn to that love. Rejoice in what he asks!

". . . for my eyes have seen your salvation, which you have prepared in the presence of all peoples, a light for revelation to the Gentiles and for glory to your people Israel."
Luke 2:30-32

Thursday, December 30
Sixth Day in the
Octave of Christmas

There was also a prophet, Anna the daughter of Phanuel. . . .
At that moment she came and began to praise God and to
speak about the child to all who were looking for the
redemption of Jerusalem. *Luke 2:36, 38*

    Anna could *see*. She could see who was before her, and what the child meant for the world. A prophet is someone who looks deeply into the world, and knows the world has something to say. She translates.

    A prophet is not fooled by the world, nor is she captured by it. She knows the world is a place to meet the presence of God. It's a "word" of God. The world is not God. The world sometimes writes for God. The world sometimes speaks for God.

    The world doesn't need to be worshipped, just respected and listened to. Like Anna. Love only God. Listen to the world.

**And the world and its desire
are passing away, but
those who do the will
of God live forever.**
        1 John 2:17

Friday, December 31
Seventh Day in the Octave of Christmas

The love of the Father is not in those who love the world; for all that is in the world—the desire of the flesh, the desire of the eyes, the pride in riches—comes not from the Father but from the world. And the world and its desire are passing away, but those who do the will of God live forever.
1 John 2:15b-17

Desire. Attachment. These things can draw us away from the love we are asked to receive and to give. The tradition of John calls them "the world." They are to be encountered respectfully, for they are powerful.

Part of understanding the Christmas mystery is welcoming a God who is so freely generous. It challenges us to examine all the "un-freedom" in our lives, and all the subtle oppressions and manipulations we use to capture the love we desire. There is a contemporary word for a person who is entrapped by a cycle of desire and attachment, who "loves the world," in John's language: *Addict*.

Christmas is the program of recovery.

[Step Three] **In the beginning was the Word, and the Word was with God, and the Word was God. . . . What has come into being in him was life. . . .** *John 1:1, 3b-4a*

Saturday, January 1
Mary, Mother of God

And because you are children, God has sent the Spirit of his Son into our hearts, crying, "Abba! Father!" So you are no longer a slave but a child, and if a child then also an heir, through God. *Galatians 4:6–7*

We need to constantly assert who this Jesus is, because our lives depend on it. We celebrate this feast as another way of saying "truly God, and truly human." Without one or the other, we are lost.

For this entire week, the scriptures have been opening up the mystery of Christmas to us. The Word-made-flesh-for-us speaks from every corner of the human experience.

God, keep our eyes opening wider. Let our ears hear the more subtle word. Let our hearts await true tenderness.

That's it, isn't it? We need Mary's eyes, Mary's ears, Mary's heart.

But Mary treasured all these words, and pondered them in her heart. *Luke 2:19*

Sunday, January 2
Epiphany of the Lord

Arise, shine; for your light has come, and the glory of the Lord has risen upon you. *Isaiah 60:1*

The first morning unshackled, eyes with sight restored, the reuniting of estranged hearts: this is the gift of Christ made manifest. How often life seems dimmed, remote, far from the beauty of this bright day. The Christmas season continues to open its mystery. The solid creation to which the world had become so accustomed, the commonplace of flesh and blood, rock and wood, is now revealed as the dwelling place of God.

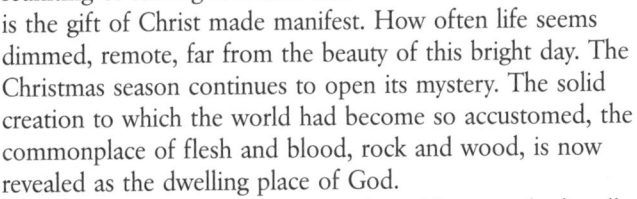

Our slumbering hearts are awakened by a mother's call, "Arise! My Word is made flesh!" And we, still half asleep, stumble out into a morning ablaze with God's light.

A clear hide
　　Of ice like an extra bark on every
　　　　Stem and branch catches each light.
Therefore no light is lost: sky light,
　　Lamp light, light from windows, moon.
　　　　And in this glaze all light is white.

The frisson at first seeing it:
　　You gasp, suck in a surprise of frozen air.
　　　　For a minute you can not breathe
So much cold beauty stops you, stops your heart
　　That you forget you are cold.

from "Ice Storm"

Monday, January 3
Christmas Weekday

By this you know the Spirit of God: every spirit that confesses Jesus Christ has come in the flesh is from God, and every spirit that does not confess Jesus is not from God.
1 John 4:2

After celebrating Christ's manifestation, we turn back to Christmas Day, when we knelt at the proclamation of this mystery of our faith.

In the FLESH. Touchable, knowable, desirable flesh. Some people don't like this idea, and find it troubling. Peculiarly, they find the idea of Christ in bread and cup less troubling. In some ways, the Eucharist is a bit more manageable because we can encounter Christ on our own schedule. But PEOPLE? And the thought that they would have something to do with my salvation?

> *You are a word God utters to me,*
> *In the syntax of your eyes,*
> *In the dialect of your hands.*
> *You are God's syllables,*
> *His breath like a ghost in the shape of a thought.*
> *And in the economy of His speech*
> *You are a little air between his lips.*
>   from "You Are a Word God Utters to Me"

Tuesday, January 4
Saint Elizabeth Ann Seton

Beloved, let us love one another, because love is from God; everyone who loves is born of God and knows God. Whoever does not love does not know God, for God is love. God's love was revealed among us in this way: God sent his only Son into the world so that we might live through him.
1 John 4:7-9

This is God's word; God's final, irrevocable word.

It's more than a word. It's a shout. It's a song. It's what God has been trying to tell us from the beginning.

God has tried to tell us this in so many ways. When Saint Elizabeth Ann Seton gazed intently at the tabernacle, she heard that word. "He is there!" she cried.

Listen.
Food when you were hungry.

Listen.
Abundance where there was only a little.

Listen.

. . . and he had compassion for them, because they were like sheep without a shepherd; and he began to teach them many things.
Mark 6:34

WEDNESDAY, JANUARY 5
SAINT JOHN NEUMANN

God is love, and those who abide in love abide in God, and God abides in them. *1 John 4:16b*

This beautiful excerpt from scripture doesn't need many words of prose.

Say it five times, pausing for five seconds between each recitation, every day for the rest of your life.

This is the connection of Christmas. It is profound. It cannot be undone. It touches every aspect of your body, soul and spirit. It is the recovery of what was lost and the promise of what will be.

> *Then Christ walked me*
> *Into a poem he had made.*
>
> *It was a garden.*

from "When Christ Comes"

Thursday, January 6
Christmas Weekday

"The Spirit of the Lord is upon me, because he has anointed me to bring good news to the poor. He has sent me to proclaim release to the captives and recovery of sight to the blind, to let the oppressed go free, to proclaim the year of the Lord's favor." *Luke 4:18-19*

> The poor.
> > The captives.
> > > The blind.
> > > > The oppressed.
>
> *Why these?*

Why, at Christmastime, would I be prompted by the Spirit to go to people such as these? To bring them presents? Not likely.

We prepared for his coming in earnestness this Advent. We celebrated the feasts, we welcomed the folks, we praised, we glorified. We did everything we were asked to do! So, what more does God want?

God has been enormously generous this Christmas. But the Spirit is prompting *me* to give another gift. Wait, did he mean *present* or *presence*? Maybe I just got it wrong.

> *You are a word God utters to me,*
> *The same word always*
> *Which I do not always hear*
> *The same, not being altogether fluent in the language.*
> > from "You Are a Word God Utters to Me"

Friday, January 7
Christmas Weekday

This is the one who came by water and the blood, Jesus Christ, not with the water only, but with the water and the blood. And the Spirit is the one that testifies, for the Spirit is the truth. There are three that testify: the Spirit and the water and the blood, and these three agree. *1 John 5:6-8*

This is a good season to talk about Jesus, to share what you know. As you find yourself full of the knowledge of the love God has shown you in Jesus, don't just keep it to yourself. Let the Spirit speak! Testify!

He woke me up this mornin',
    and he clothed me in my right mind!

He made a way when there was no way!

He's my rock in a weary land!

I once was lost . . . but now am found.

No one can resist this love, if you share it gently, not trying to coerce. *You* are water and blood! Testify!

And this is the testimony: God gave us eternal life, and this life is in His Son. *John 5:11*

Saturday, January 8
Christmas Weekday

And we know that the Son of God has come and has given us understanding so that we may know him who is true; and we are in him who is true, in his Son Jesus Christ. He is the true God and eternal life. *1 John 5:20*

The deep purpose of his coming, and the deep purpose of this season, is to draw us more perfectly into the life of God. Jesus is the way into God. Christmas, with its images and even its choice of scripture, can subtly suggest that it's fine just "to get to know Jesus." But Jesus wants us to go further; he wants us to be where he lives and to know what he knows.

The Advent and Christmas seasons are filled with journeys—down hammered out roads through the desert, from the rural town to bustling city, from dangerous homeland to foreign country, from rough wood manger to rough wood cross. God is taking us somewhere.

Issued time and again in water and blood, the love of God is made present in the flesh that we might see it, contemplate it, and desire it all the more. God's hope for each of us: that we might want God as much as God wants us.

> **Little children, keep yourselves from idols.**
> *1 John 5:21*

Sunday, January 9
Baptism of the Lord

> Here is my servant, whom I uphold, my chosen, in whom my soul delights. *Isaiah 42:1a*

Christ is revealed as flesh and blood, in poverty and with purpose. This "second Epiphany" fills out the first: it is indeed a human being who is the beloved of God. The word of God is a person, and ever shall be.

What I find most frightening, most challenging, and most humbling, is that you and I are revealed on this day as well. God's servants, whom God upholds. With work to be done!

You are a word God utters to me,
In the syntax of your eyes,
In the dialect of your hands.
You are God's syllables,
His breath like a ghost in the shape of a thought,
And in the economy of His speech,
You are a little air between his lips.

You are a word God utters to me.
And I am a word with which He answers you.

from "You Are a Word God Utters to Me"

ADVANCE RESERVATION FORM

Living the Days of Advent and the Christmas Season 2005

This collection of daily reflections–a perennial favorite of Paulist Press readers–is an ideal way to prepare for Advent. Instead of being a month of increasing stress, with the help of this book Advent can be a quiet season reflection on the miracle that God has come to us, will come, and is already with us now. For each day the author includes a selection from scripture or the divine office, a brief meditation, and a prayer. Together they help the hassles and trivialities of the season fall away to reveal the real and unchanging meaning beneath.

The 2005 edition:
- runs from the First Sunday of Advent to the Baptism of the Lord, noting feast days and holy days
- invites us to open our hearts and eyes to the in-breaking of Immanuel, Jesus, into our lives; it is a time to look at the ordinary moments of life and see within them the extraordinary presence of God
- comes in the handy tear-out, page-a-day format.

Reserve Your Copy Today!

Please send me _____ copy(ies) of: **Living the Days of Advent and the Christmas Season 2005 #0-8091-4271-6 @ $3.95 ea.**

Please include applicable sales tax, and postage and handling ($3.50 for first $20 plus 50¢ for each additional $10 ordered)—check or money order only payable to **Paulist Press**.

Enclosed is my check or money order in the amount of $ _____

Name _____

Position _____

Institution _____

Street _____

City/State/Zip_____

Phone # _____

For more information or to receive a free catalog of our publications, contact us at:

Paulist Press™ 997 Macarthur Blvd., Mahwah, N.J. 07430 • 1-800-218-1903
FAX 1-800-836-3161 • E-MAIL: info@paulistpress.com • www.paulistpress.com